PARALLAX

Wesleyan New Poets

PARALLAX

Maureen Mulhern

Wesleyan University Press
Middletown, Connecticut

Copyright © 1986 by Maureen Mulhern

"Candelia" received the 1984 Ruth Lake Memorial Award
from the Poetry Society of America

Library of Congress Cataloging-in-Publication Data
Mulhern, Maureen, 1957–
  Parallax.

  (Wesleyan new poets)
  I. Title. II. Series.
PS3563.U393P3 1986   811'.54   85-22750
ISBN 0-8195-2130-2 (alk. paper)
ISBN 0-8195-1131-5 (pbk.: alk. paper)

All inquiries and permissions requests should be addressed
to the Publisher, Wesleyan University Press, 110 Mt.
Vernon Street, Middletown, Connecticut 06457.

Distributed by Harper & Row Publishers, Keystone
Industrial Park, Scranton, Pennsylvania 18512.

Manufactured in the United States of America

FIRST EDITION

Wesleyan New Poets

For my parents . . .

Contents

PARALLAX

Skating

Over Sinoway's pond the snag of skates
Dragged rough lines across the crust.

I imagined crayfish in hibernation,
Their pewter spines curled in frozen viscous

Sacs and bubbles while hockey pucks
Sent shadows over them like tiny spheres

Whizzing out of orbit. I spun crookedly,
Snow catching on my eyelashes

As I stumbled, pulled by a mottled glow
Of fish below the ice, their opaque,

Greenish skin as fine as rice paper, mouths
Stuck in perpetual loops. I circled

And etched cuneiform runes, scrambled
Messages to wood-hued owls who took

Refuge in Sinoway's barn. (Their tight,
oval chests beneath the feathers, cold.) Cider

Fermented in enormous vats and apples
All summer long waited listlessly like

People in bus stations. But the winter
Was an Appaloosa, bruised white and grey,

Its mane, cream turning pale against the sky.
At night, I dreamed of clear, red planets

Eclipsing thinner disks, shifting
Like ocular cells on all sides; featureless

Faces bobbed for eye space while I clung
To the basket of a hot-air balloon

And felt the world obliquely tip away, sliding
Further and further to where I am now.

Candelia

Once I'd walk from one end of the living–
Room to another, the medication took hold
And I'd turn into sand;
Particle against particle,

A slow-motion storm that always seemed to drift
Further away. I'd arrive
At the other side, a little changed,
Listening to the breaths of creatures

Barely visible. The lizards
Slipping beneath hibiscus leaves
Were oddly human in their muteness.
And in my blurred sight

Palmettos snagged across the walls,
Mapping out haphazard trails.
In the hospital's room,
As I tried to read, my eyes could not

Leave the words *humming–*
Birds, dragonflies; when they lifted up
From the page, a balm of wings
Swirled beneath my pillow

In a column of dust, sand and sun.
Next to me, an old woman
Was brought in from a Nursing Home
With a Condensed Reader's Digest,

Small black purse, comb, slippers,
Rosaries and glasses. The blood
That poured from her, night and day,
Gathered into pans, the sound of rain

Made slow and magnified.
When I left, I leaned down
Over her face, my shadow moving
Between us; her eyes were distant and specific

In that half-light. It was June
When the early morning's poultice broke
Between a word and its sound, a body
And its death. The memory I have

Of that woman is of her strength and silence,
How language was a forgotten thing,
Her relatives apologizing
For the inconvenience of it all.

Daydreaming at the Beach

. . . just before I finally fall asleep
My body scatters the dark particles
Like a shoal dispersed in the wake of waves.

Sea gulls let go prehistoric shrieks,
Bursts of violet-grey. Past the horizon
I imagine dolphins and whales,
Sun splashing against skin
As they surface, curving behind my eyes.
When I released my body
From all its fears, made love
With freedom, such complete light passing
Through two bodies; a moment
Of suspension, before a wave leans
Into the next wave, descending back, a slight
Vertigo of gravity between us.
Your eyelids, when I touched them, turned
To pale moths of gold.
To envy gulls and sparrows,
Their gibberish, their simple lives.
Through my lashes, the sun, a straw hat,
Thrown dizzily into the sky.
I feel the soft, incomprehensible
Locution of the wind, the birds flying
Through my ribs.

Die Forelle

Tucked between the pages of "The Trout"
An unopened letter, postmarked April.
It's late September now; six months
This letter has lain next to the trout's song

Whose notes, like liquid hooks and tiny
Whittled spines, squirmed impatiently
For resuscitation and gravity to release them
Up. The notes swam like tadpoles

Between miniature lightning bolts, straying
Telephone poles, ascending b b b b b's,
A few upside-down golf clubs,
Others with the curve of high-heeled shoes,

Legs and eyes of insects, dangling, not quite
Fully assembled. All the while the letter remained
Jammed between the pages
Like a silent tongue. In dated language,

The refrain, with lilting, false naïveté, sang
Of how the trout will "never be taken
Tho'long he persevere." I wondered for a moment
About the sender of the letter, of the letter

Itself, which by now had taken on a life
Of diminished singularity, and all the reasons
Why it had been left
Unopened in the death song of a trout.

Out of some vague, distant, atavistic
And not yet defined respect,
I took that letter home, mailed it
And as if it had anything to do with me,

I watched it drift away
Like a fish or a refugee, not knowing
The circumstances of how it would be received
And brought back

Once again into this scrambled world.

Edging

Across the lake a wire of sun
Climbs slowly up a heron's leg;

Clamped in the bird's beak, a fish
Glistens, twisting at the tail.

Stones burst open;
Over them, water spreads

A cold, translucent hand. Brittle
Planks of sunlight lean

Against sea-grape trees and blue
Pines stooping to their roots.

Even by day the moon ticks on,
Its expression hardening

Beneath marmoreal flesh.
Flies swoon, metallic music

Trails behind, they carve
Wide loops through the air.

Everywhere, muscles churn out
Of necessity, edging

To a darkness they assume is light.

Matinal

Snow all night against the windowpanes
Charted haphazard maps; leaf-sized shadows
Sailing lazily over your skin
Pulled us through a shroud of warmth. Morning,
We just barely felt the stars uncurl
As they trailed in our room a pale incense
Of light. Discovering love that gave
Way as easily as ice rafts and floes
Dislocate in slow motion, we heard
Leaves and pine needles spiral weightlessly
Below the ground; each breath you took went
Close inside me, unfolding in mauve air,
Belonging no more to your body,
But to where it centers and unravels
Outside its own sound. Every touch
And kiss, we felt the long inhalation
Of spruce and ash as they gathered round
Beads of sun threading along their bare spines.
A few startled and bewildered crows
Expected new weather, fraying sparrows
Sensed signs of a fifth, unnamed season,
And for months that haunted New England house
Filled with the haze of our touches; ghosts
Harvested smoke from candles as we would
Still save from each other the random
Circles of a compass turning us through
That which has become out of our reach
And all of that we have never let go.

After Rain, What Entropy Appears

After rain, pulling pollen from the still wet
And scattered thistles, bees dance

In a slow electric blur
Of sound; trailing the thin white threads,

Their throats release a haphazard weave.
After rain, in the sun's new green, desire

Unloosens at the slightest, most honed
Inhalation of sight. And the moths, they are not self–

Contained and intent
On following those whittled tracks of space

Each orbit issues from the air.
I'm convinced there's no clear way to chart

Exhilaration or defeat; the parallax
Where each thing moves out

Of its own range itself cannot be
Pinned down. To trace the edges sight leaves,

Not the crisp patterns fashioning themselves
Indiscreetly into view,

But where a wing separates the air, a new element
Takes shape from what surrounds it; as the eye

Adjusts, it too becomes more
And then less divisible from that birth.

Lost in Italy

Four years old. I watch pale backs
Sink into water, such familiar
Immortal parents. Almost
Automatically, I turn the other way.

Like the pupil of a cat's eye
Brushed by light, the horizon tightens
To a thin wire and I am pulled
Into danger.

A nomad. I possess the sand.
Bronze faces beneath parasols,
Liquidy voices stretch out to me:
"Su vieni, piccola, vieni qui."

I back away, strung
To an opalescent sight
Of twenty orphans led by nuns.
In gauzy white robes,

They float along the beach
Like illuminated gulls.
An unnoticed intruder, I follow
Their cloud for miles.

Then, my grandmother,
A fierce goddess in her white
Bathing cap, her head as smooth
As a light bulb, emerges

From the sea, her arms
Like strands of coral, lips fuming
With lives of their own,
Saves me, saves me . . .

The Lake

As we row across,
Blisters on our palms
Rise like barnacles.
We imagine we can hear
A metallic hiss
From underwater plants
As they grope and spiral
Beneath the oars
That kick up sparks
Of water. Like a necklace
Slowly pulled, candles
Slide around us
In a circle.
Silence cracks
Against the air;
Brushing our necks
And throats, fireflies,
Dizzily exploding
Into flames,
Sting the evening's
Spreading flesh.
As we trace our fingers
Along the surface,
A few translucent fish
Nudge at us,
Their gelatin, mackerel-
Spotted eyes loom
And veer away. Turtles sink
Below the swaying
Shadow of the boat;
Their moony shells
Are etched with grids,

Pentagrams and scars.
The lake unravels
Glacial light.
I wake and a single
Silver scale drops
Like a petal
From my hair;
A talisman
Coaxing the elliptical
Space between us
To constrict
Like the veined interior
Of a fish
Whose fluted gills
Suck for air.
And I think of this
As though we were never
There at all, as though
The lake were a cataract
And mired in its haze,
We could not see
Nor break
Its vision upon us.

Palm-Reading

The dream in your hand leans
Into the life-line, fanning open
Like an underwater flower.

That region behind your eye
Where the universe rattles
An elliptical grain pinpoints

The past as whitened antlers
Cluttering a desert's sand;
The present is a firefly

Scorching trails through smoke;
The future, a blue gazelle
Gliding from its body.

As a cold fleck of moonlight
Rolls like tumbleweed
Across your palm's terrain,

You wake up
And can almost hear
The faint sound of clouds

Crashing against air.
The rain outside
Is merciless.

Under a Tundra, the Desert, the Sea

A convalescing light congeals
To shadows in the bulbs.
My grandmother's eyes turn.

Her nails, buffed to a dull,
Milky glow, like shells underwater,
Move to pull the blankets

Closer to her chin. The blankets
Slide in an avalanche, slowly
Reversed. Outside, God is still

Lying down in the spirals of a snail;
The silver rivers burn in the sun.
My grandmother is still alive

In semidarkness. We play cards.
Sea-grape trees scraping
Against the window, a spotlight

Or two from small boats, skiffs
Trailing their gauzy nets
Like trains of wedding gowns

Through the black water.
She shuffles the cards,
Embarrassed at her awkwardness.

In the morning, the night, tropical
And fat, lies exhausted,
Scattered in pieces

On the floor. A few lizards
Pulse bluish flames
Through their eyes as they wait

For relief, clouds; my grandmother
Still moves in another language,
Almost the same way.

Along the Promenade

As you sketch the bristling skyline,
The moon slinks into your hands

And sends a string of fire
Through each finger. Bees loop

Fierce invisible knots
And flare as if lit from within;

Their jagged throats
Needle out a tune. Small deaths

Unraveling bring a lavender glow
To the water's skin. Chained

By their open shadows, some caged
Poplars lean

To slivers of gravity.
Brushing the charcoal's dust

Away from your sketch,
Resolved to start again

Tomorrow, you leave,
Parting columns of thick air

That always seem to stack
Their weight against you, almost.

11/84

for Alison

The chimes' skeletal notes swung
From the wracked but still living body

Of a tree hit by lightning.
I think back to that cold November

Morning of your father's death,
How we stood beneath the sun's toxic eye,

Shivering in a field, drinking black coffee
From a thermos. Steam escaping

Briefly dispersed into brittle air.
Your father's dark wool scarf wrapped

Around you the immediate solace
Of all that was familiar . . . a warmth

You can still return to when memory's
Offerings are too many to bear.

Medulla

The sky widened like the belly of an animal
Playing dead beat-up trucks rattled
Rakes and hoes scrawny weather vanes

Twisted in the wind clods of dirt dangled
From a broom Bing Crosby crooned
A liquidacious tune about love

And pain as though honey dripped
Behind thick glass inching down I turned
Into an empty field in exile

Frost scurried off
The windshield and a bird flew
In front of me its head and neck were kind

Of hangman's hoodish only bright red
Wings black grey and white spun
As though I'd hurled it

Out of sleep to the center of a tree
It clung there against the bark exposed
Quivering like some heart's muscle

A bull's eye spewn onto a target
Trembling in a prolepsis
Of what it could not see for a moment

I considered going up to it to study
What worlds were held in those small eyes
Instead I watched it shake

Its wings and lean back to begin
Its gentle steady hammering
While snow scattered down like leaves

The Shell

I pick up a shell that I found with you
And balance it in my palm,
Its cool serrated shadow drops across
A life line that has changed again and turned
Like a compass, leading me into something other
And new. In the morning as sunlight overlapped
The corners of our room,
I'd touch your ear with my tongue and listen
To love's sounds growing singular
And quiet. (Remember, it was an early
Complacency that wound into our lives
And drew all its layers around us.) In memory
Of what we shared, I'll place this shell back
In the vague direction of its birth.

Candles in the Forest

As light uncoils
Within the smoky columns
It ignites the petals
From buds into flowers each
One beautiful and alive
Flames rise from the cups

Of magnolia blossoms
Beneath the soft whir
Of locusts as the dead speak
Their words are given flight
Above their ashes evolving
With a new lineage

We emerge bewildered
By the stacks of ghosts
That log up
Ahead of us filling the forest
With the white torches
Of their fingernails

The moist smell
Of myrrh taking root
The losses settling
Themselves the gods that have returned
To start again from what
We have left

Parallax

In the orchard, mosquitoes enter
From the night's walls like bulls
Released into a ring. Curving through trees
The wind grapples with a burlap bag
Clinging to its pinch of gravity.
Below the suspended blizzard of fruit,
As darkness folds into itself,
Crickets, with their usual hysteria,
Their urgent "but but but" voices,
Click sparks of light back
Into the moon. The wind gathers
And continues to send broken clouds
Across the sky and this life
Sliding on, far ahead of me.

On the Highway

Darkness washes away
Expressions and features

Of the people in the bus.
Like a theater crowd, they are remote

And self-contained. Moonlit barns
Slide by, their faces are as anonymous

As hitchhikers'.
The road's dividers uncoil and vanish

Beneath the bus.
Now and then something snags,

The remembrance of a dream
In which the victim, criminal and witness

Are one; its fluid structure
Falls through memory's net.

Next to me an old man
Guards a battered briefcase;

Streetlights flash dimly through his glasses.
I feel as if we are within

The belly of a fish, gliding
Aimlessly, content with its own blind travel.

A web of stars
Glints behind the window as snow

Parachutes down.
All the unfinished beginnings

Come back to me now; my regrets
Amble away without purpose,

Neither hopeful, nor discouraged,
Like animals, indistinguishable in the dark,

Which, having discovered no food
By the roadside, turn

And wander into the woods.

Cloth Stars

For my mother

I think of a star sewn loosely
To your coat, its grey shadow
Pinned under your skin, and of constellations

Seeping through the morning sky in Jerusalem,
Each leaf of Gethsemane's olive trees
Dipped in the silver blood of mist.

Now, where you are, the sea
Is a blue and ragged scythe, a thumbnail
View of enormity spreading past a talismanic

Clicking of waves, a vague
Settlement into tomorrow, where never the small
Surroundings that close in on you

Are enough to grow. Little
By little, I break the net of amnesia
You have woven across your past.

Your life moves into mine at the same rate
I move away. The collected moments
When you would disappear for a night:

No one knew where you went or when
You would come back.
I imagine the clouds turning over Vienna

In a sleep of singed snow.
And I see your grandparents still living
Under the illusion of safety,

Drinking thick Turkish coffee
From thimble-sized cups
While the furnace lights up the faces

Of relatives I can know
Only by name or photograph; the lost
Emerge haphazardly.

Now, outside your window,
The moon grazes the sea
And rolls away, threading a circle

Of small copper flames across
The water. Moving just out of reach,
Angelfish that glide like translucent hands

Are bewildered guides who return
From where you have left, and still,
You speak of your childhood as if it were

An animal trailing you, not quite
Visible in the shadows; the strength
I need to step out of your past.

Winter

The weightlessness
Of the moon, an ephemerid's
Wing pinned to a web, a single

Light syllable
That has managed to slip
Out of the sky's violet mouth. You float

Down the long ice of an owl's cry
Lifting a cargo
Of alchemy that never changes.

Provisional

Around me, decisions sprawled on rocks
And leaves. Shadows often fell across
The fountain's fish below, darkening
The coins once tossed in for luck. A love
As true as all mistakes would allow,
As all regretted blunderings,
Lead to me holding you one night
Of your married life. I did not know enough
To know fear, to feel the body tensing
At a touch so desired. That tenderness
Has not left, and as I say this now,
And you are living out a life
I no longer wish to know, whatever loss
Has taken over moves slowly, and love,
I'll tell you, it does not go.

At Sea

Noon here. Bleached air filters from the sky. Even in the o of twelve noon, turning counterclockwise, the starfish simultaneously circle their individual plates. Slowly, although calcified in orbit, the scrape of their arms on the porcelain plates keeps time. There are five plates, five starfish, twenty-five arms. Noon here. Bleached air filters from the sky. Even in the o of twelve noon, turning counterclockwise, the starfish simultaneously circle their individual plates. Maybe there will be time. Clearly, the plates are on a wood table, the wood table is on a boat, the boat is anchored in the middle of the ocean. At night, the starfish crawl up the sides of the boat and settle onto their plates. They remain motionless until noon. When viewed from above, the edges of the plates around the starfish gleam like marmoreal haloes. Shadow-scraps, glistening with brine, serve as garnish while seaweed, which had already been demystified ages ago, lounges on the floor of the boat. The starfish are nestled in their plates and the plates have long forgotten the way they used to be. Patiently, diligently, the starfish circle, trying to connect the ends of o. (Counterclockwise means having to turn left, and these starfish, so accustomed to that direction, are wary of turning otherwise because to do so would click them closer toward one o'clock, an unheard-of hour at sea.) Still, it is noon and the starfish are circling their plates and the seaweed, as usual, is laughing.

The Firewalkers

Lankadas' villagers wait and watch
The others who all year fast
In preparation. There was no confusion
As the icons, squeezed in
Revolving fists, St. Constantine, St. Helen,

Swirled safely above
The coals Sotirios Liouris crossed
With calm ecstasy. Nine cows gazed
Behind a ring of wire; his wife
Looked on nearby. A few cameras

Anointed him and the others
With clicks of recognition snapping
Like iguana tongues.
Around them, mountains a thousand
Times larger than the icons,

Shrunk and assumed a distant
Look of bewilderment. Sacrificial
Bulls writhed from their ashes;
Pyres three days old smoldered with oil.
A circle of gnarled olive trees,

Shrouded in immolations
Of slow green light, celebrated those
Who carry in the cool urns of their bodies
A faith that cinders will provide
For the spirit to burn through.

Lago Mar

The hostess, Pearl, her champagne
Hair catching the sun, waves
At us with the swish of a charm-

Braceleted wrist.
My mother and I sit beneath
A yellow umbrella,

Drinking hot tea, mildly
Out of place. Sparrows
Dance at our feet

Like jumping beans, nervously,
They hop for crumbs. Around us,
Orange birds-

Of-paradise rise like tiny flames
From clay urns, lizards cling
To brittle stems, their quartz

Eyes darken, staring. Across
The terrace, a ragged
Circle of lime

Twists in tonic, a life raft
Caught in a whirlpool.
The ocean breathes, disrupting

The dreamy undulations
Of bathers who float like flotsam.
My mother and I

Brush sand from our legs
As we leave; the umbrella seems slightly
Askew and rusted. Pearl smiles,

Her pale hair glistens
In sunlight. Behind her, the ocean
Sprawls like a polar bear, belly up.

The Wait

I should have seen it as a sign.
The pale blood splattered faintly
On the walls. Vapors uncoiled

Disseminating fragments
On the attic's floor. Your oxygen's
Clear molecules clinking

As they followed one another up some custom–
Made spiral stairs. The noon sun trapped
In jagged spines of icicles.

The eventual disappearance
Of one who spent a lifetime
Trying to figure out the ocean's vague geometry.

        Through all the nights of others
And their small promises, the rituals
Spiraling beyond their birth,

After so many years,
I turned back, after the anger
Had long been worn away,

Though not far enough, to appease
Your loss. Always in the background, the ocean's
Dark iridescent shells battered through the waves

In a perpetual baptismal wash
Of false beginnings. In memory
Even now you bring in a few of the indelible

Regrets that I have planned to leave
At the ocean's edge. I shall watch
Among the reeds as brine takes them

In minerals beyond recognition;
As changed as you are,
I will be prepared for your return.

With Love

Around us the wide floes began
To tear apart, sending their slow music
Of dissent in horizontal limbs.
But then you slipped and that cold water

Took you in. Your hands, marbled from age,
Grasped at the sliding edges of the ice.
I pulled you up, heard you breathe
The same words whose sounds I'd known

Almost thirty years before. When you rescued me
In a warm, foreign climate,
Brine glistened on your darkened skin,
The sunlight wavering across your teeth

Struck those words exchanged between us.
And the ocean, with all its answers,
Moved out of reach, enormous and fragile,
As unreachable as you are now.

From the Country

for Linda

It was summertime
And I'd touch the leaves thinking
How beautiful they were

Wearing caterpillars like jewelry
Some nights his hands
Seemed to burst out of themselves

Fleshy animals
Turtles without their shells
They crawled along my body while I froze

Saying to myself *he needs*
This he needs this
All I could think about

When the hours got smaller
And further away
Was the translucent pink

Of fingernails and clean white linen
And how Andrei's eyes swam behind his glasses
Like grey fish in a clouded pond

He was so blind lord
He needed a special cane
It scared me the way it reached

From this world into another
Bouncing off a curb
Without even touching it

It sent an electricity so fine
Only Andrei could feel
He once told me of a woman he loved

Years ago she was blind
From birth I think he wanted to buy her
A jade necklace told me how she asked

The shopgirl to describe exactly
The color of all the jade necklaces
Said there were at least twenty

I imagine her fingers moving over
The beads like delicate creepers
As the shopgirl says no

This one is darker more olive
Or this is bluer almost
Clear sort of turquoise

They were there for hours
And when he finally got her the necklace
She was exhilarated so satisfied

He felt left out mystified
With my eyes closed
I can still see the morning's

Sunlight wavering
Through vials of insulin on his desk
Piles of dirty clothes

A smell of oranges and dust
And sadness and loss it took months
Before I saw how I loved

His memories more than him
And for a second I could see
He was old he was an old man

I didn't love it was then
When I'd begin to wish
To be whole again and be inside

The soft slush of my mother
Where I'd watch her hands
Covering the pink globe

Lightly beneath her fingers
As I curled up and slept
For what seemed like forever

Night by Cool Water

A few boats sigh and inhale
With a gentle clang; the wind
Unspools its blue tongue
And curls around the evening's waist.

Crickets and aquatic bugs
Murmur in controlled, slightly frantic tones;
Their voices are electric galaxies of sound.
Lightning sprays x-ray ribbons

Across the sky; vertebrae, spires, masts
Flare up in a green fluorescent glow.
As thick as tar, light pours
Back to the surface of things, oozing

From the waves, a sense
That time vanishes; this life
Sways on the mercurial ring
Of each breath the boats release.

The Quarry

Above the quarry the moon sweats in its bath
Of loneliness and boredom. As a child, I watched my mother

Trace lines around her eyes;
In the mirror, those lines seemed to me

Like estuaries on a map. Lingering in fluid
Warmth, the moon's aura seeps and spreads

Like Betadine around a wound. The quarry's water is oily
At night, and a few innocuous shapes appear

To drift like stitches that, long
Unremembered, return back beneath healed skin.

Burning Boat

The Coast Guard's helicopter
Hovers like an octopus
Above the smoke. Buoyant

From wave after wave,
As slick as black pearls
Or manatees, passengers

Tread through moonlight.
It twists a few thin arms
Around their moving shapes:

Tendrils and ropes spill down
In a net, making the rescue quick.
Later, a muffled crack of flames

Against water, oil secretes
Matted hot perfume.
Threads rise as though the boat below

Released the souls of all those
Who were unable to lift, hand
Over drained hand,

Through inverted spiracles of air
Ruptured from above, or grasp
Plastic wreaths tossed at them

One by one, and pull back up
To a world already swollen
With arbitrary wreaths, random fire.

Apology

Like O'Keeffe's deserts, littered
With brittle bones, I built a field
That collected gestures and intentions
Never pushed far enough away
From their source. A night
When the moon's dark grazed face lit up
In a lavender glow, I released the field,
Its habitual pull of gravity
And the anchoring fear of losing
What one thinks one is. The bones
Rose like doves and turned the sky
Into a frenzied wheel. Entering
Renunciation, at last I can offer you
This stunned bird to hold, to set free.

Ménage

You may see this as a house
Where pipes curve like swans' necks
And feathers peel, where blood
That seeps is seeping blood,

Where grief takes off
Its sweater
And lies down by the hearth
Waiting for shadows to perform.

(*Ahh,* says the soul as it basks outside
In the night's eucalyptus tree.)
This may have the feel
Of a house, but look:

One corner is lit with a pyramid
Of baby teeth; and unrequited desire
Has left on the windowpanes
Fresh fingerprints in dust.

You will not fail to hear
Walls whispering behind your back
Secrets that they claim to know
In sounds so hushed

You'll think you made them up;
Or the attic's thin and spiraled voice
Telling you vanilla
Is an orchid an orchid an orchid

Until the o of orchid leaves
Impressions in the air.
You may visit here again. Remember
The floors, how they move like rafts.

—

Equinox

I hear the ticking that uncoils in the belly
Of a scorpion as it scuttles
Not beneath the sand
In your mind, but curling
In the desert, anonymously. Where night
Tastes as bitter as a walnut
There is a sound of a spider, breathing.
I have no use for nothing, for all the pale
Petals of absences opening around us
Like unimportant mistakes.
I enter a leopard's eye
In sound, in play; the resinous
Pool, where you and I
Take off our shadows like molten skins
And touch
The evening, is a living mink.

Incubus Idolum

Imbrued in a bitter thanatoidal slime
All those crocodiles
With crenated tails looping
Out of the water where my grandmother
Had fallen walking
Straight into the danger

I saved her I tell you I dove in
And groped through that saurian mud
Where tiny newts tried to pry
Under my eyes which I had cowardly kept
Closed the whole time
I felt the weight of her shoulders

The soggy sweater tearing
Against coral the heaviness of her head
In my arms as I struggled up
To the surface
She was breathing some slow
Metronomical breaths

Her dark near black eyes open
Staring at something so large
That I could not see I said it's all right
You'll live you'll live you'll live
And she did
I'm telling you she did

Recovery

In the early humid stasis
Of recovery, memory reminds itself
That it is all you have. Your body

Is one step ahead and fear is only
A pale cologne lifting
To the ceiling. You dissolve

Into a field where snowflakes needle
Against a Palomino's flank;
Each filigree melts through its flesh,

They descend to liquid, moving, always
Into their other elements.
From behind a frozen willow tree,

A girl in a red down jacket
With a pair of skates thrown
Across one shoulder, watches closely,

Her eyes sift the winter light; somehow
She has altered in a way you may
Never know. Waking, it is night

And you can see the moon
Teetering on its stalk of gravity.
A state of mind, the seasons are

Conjured through an act of will.
But it's June, there's little chance
You'll return to this place again.

All Summer Long

Frogs stared up at us
From old glass
Mayonnaise jars
With jagged holes
Punctured in the lids
Like stars hammered
One by one into the sky
Some boys set fire
To a matchbox
Stuffed with caterpillars
That tiny coffin curled
And sizzled to the ground
Like Houdini's fingers
Their second selves climbed
Miraculous ladders of air
For a whole summer
We tried to name things
That defied being caged
From palm to palm
While we listened closely
To the clear sound and precision
Of a robin's egg
As it leaned into the dark
Hollow of its nest
Those lives left us
Containing things
We couldn't name
June July and August
Were three salamanders
Swimming away

About the Author

Maureen Mulhern was born in Birmingham, lived in
Worcester, England, and emigrated to the United States
in 1964. She grew up in North Haven, Connecticut, and
has lived in New York, Florida, Iowa, and Massachusetts.
She received a B.A. from Sarah Lawrence College (1980)
and an M.F.A. from the University of Iowa (1983). She
lives in New York City. This is her first book.

About the Book

Parallax was composed in Bembo by G & S Typesetters
of Austin, Texas. It was printed on 60 lb. Miami Book
Vellum and bound by Kingsport Press of Kingsport,
Tennessee. Design by Joyce Kachergis Book Design
and Production of Bynum, North Carolina.

Wesleyan University Press, 1986.